Best Wishes
from Bonnie Smyth
FLORIDA KEYS

Blinken, Pete and Polly

Blinken Pete and Polly

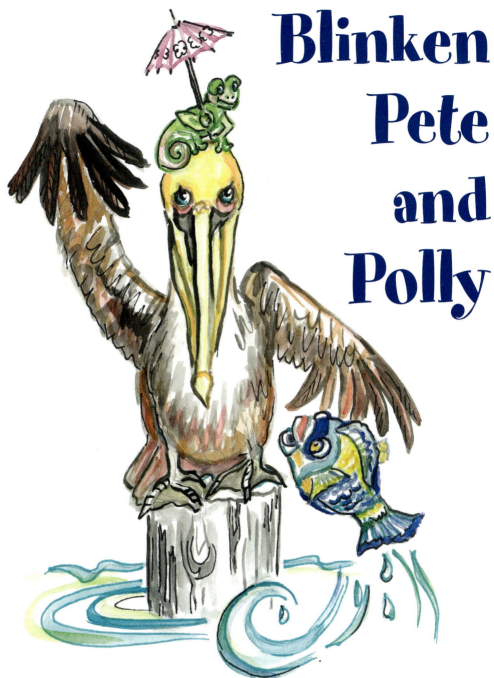

Tales in Verse, With Activities
Bonnie Staryk

SeaStory Press

Blinken, Pete and Polly

© 2013 by Bonnie Staryk

All rights reserved

Reproduction of this book or any part thereof is prohibited, except for quotation for review purposes, without express permission of the author and publisher.

Printed in Hong Kong

ISBN 978-1-936818-39-6
LCCN 2013930794

SeaStory Press
305 Whitehead St. #1
Key West. Florida 33040
www.seastorypress.com

Dedicated to:

Bode

Alyssa

and

Victoria

"You make me proud. Enjoy being you."

Table of Contents

Meet Blinken, Pete and Polly	1
Pete, the pelican	3
A lizard named Blinken	15
Polly Parrotfish	22
More fun together	30
Learn to rhyme	47
About the author	55

Pete, the Pelican,
Blinken, the Lizard
and Polly, the Parrotfish
are fun and funny
to make your day sunny.

Come with me and you will see.

Pete

A pelican called Pete
said he had performed
a fantastic feat.

"I dove so deep,
I didn't come up for a week!"

Said his bird friend, Fred,
"If that were true, you'd be dead."
                    (Hee Hee)

Pete shuffled his webbed feet.
Then he said,
"I flew so high, I touched the sky!"

"There you go again
story telling." said Fred.
"Pete, your tales sure are
an entertaining treat,

But under water for a week
you really can't stay"-

"Nor did you perform an impossible flight display."

Pete hid his eyes under his wings. He was sad and feeling bad...

"Just one more thing," added Fred. "There is no one better than you as my Pal Pelican."

"And you dive and fly
as well as any bird can.
You don't need to impress.
I'm happy with you
doing much less."

That evening, Pete watched the sunset with his friend, Fred.

Nothing else needed to be said.

Blinken

A lizard named Blinken
one day was a'think'n,
"I've got only one spot on my tail...
And look entirely too pale."

So he laid in the sun,
till he was quite done.
He freckled his hide...

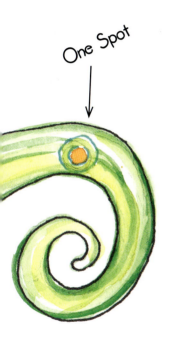

One Spot

And all joking aside,
was the most fried looking lizard
to be seen far and wide!

Blinken felt so hot
a lemonade he got.
A little bit he sipped,
then, into it, his tail he dipped!

"Aaaah..."
Offers Blinken,
 "Want some lizardade?"

Let's say, "No thank you,"
because we know how it's made.

Stay cool, Blinken.

Polly

Polly Parrotfish wondered
why she couldn't talk.
She bubbled and bubbled
but never got so much as a squawk.

Thought Sam Clam, "How silly-ish
for a featherless fish."
But through the waters Polly flew
with the sea as her sky
and the coral and weeds
her jungle passing by.

Showing her bright colors on her iridescent skin,
she pretended a parrot
really was a kin...

Till the stars in the sand were
shadowed by the night...

Sunken Ship
(Maybe Treasure
on board?)

Pete, Polly and Blinken say,
"Thanks for coming
where palm trees sway.
We hope to see you another day."

Or...

Do you have time for more fun together?

More Fun

Oh goody.
Then you can answer
some questions.

Says Polly Parrot Fish, "If
you looked at the pages...

...and read the words in the book, this will be fun."

Question 1.
What type of coral in the ocean sounds really smart?

Blinken says,
"Use your brain and you will think of the answer."

Silly Blinken,
you gave the answer away.
Yes, it is BRAIN CORAL.

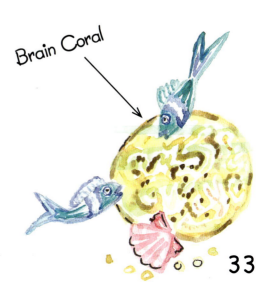

Brain Coral

Good Job.
More?
OK.

Question 2.
What is the name of
a fruit that grows
on a palm tree?

"Ah, that's easy,"
says Pete, the Pelican.

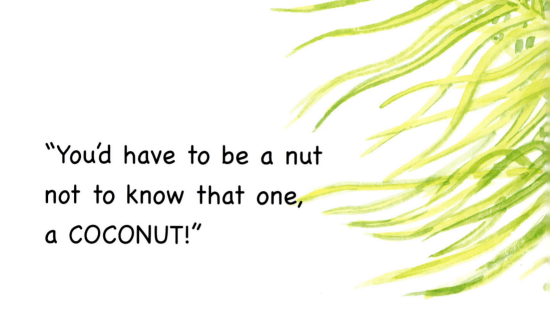

"You'd have to be a nut not to know that one, a COCONUT!"

Yummy

Question 3.

What kind of water tastes like salt?

"If you said salt water," burbled Polly, "you'd be right, but you could say the OCEAN or the SEA.

"I swim in the ocean.
I swim in the sea.
I like salt water.
It's right for me."

and a salty taste in your mouth.

We're almost done.
You've done well. Right?

Question 4.
What is an island?

"I fly over them," says Pete,
flapping his wings.

"I swim around them," says Polly, wiggling her tail.

"I live on one," says Blinken, "in The Florida Keys where there are over a hundred islands!"

Some islands are BIG.
Some islands are small.

Here is a picture of a pretty island

One more question... The last one.

Question 5.
Do YOU live on an island?

"That's what I thought," says Pete.

"Right," says Blinken and Polly.
"We like where you live too."

Toy Boat

Rhyming

Now, if you don't drift away,
take the time to learn to rhyme.

YOU CAN!
We'll tell you how.
Quickly turn the page.

Lazy Lucy

Float

That was pretty quick!
I'll bet you noticed some words in the book ended with the same sound.
That is rhyming.
Like: Funny/Sunny,
       Boat/Float

You can rhyme words too.

CAT rhymes with _____

clue

Create Rhymes With Blinken

(Add your own rhyming words)

Out in the sun

Blinken has lots of _____

When he climbs a tree,

There is a lot to _____

A lizard like Blinken has a tail
and a boat can have a _____

Too much sun can cause a burn.
It was a hard lesson
for Blinken to _____

You're a Poet!

(That's what they call someone
who rhymes.)

And you can write your own
rhyming stories.
Maybe someone you know would
like to help you.
You can ask.
We hope the answer is "Yes."

Draw some pictures too
or you can do it later.

We had a nice time.
"Bye," say Pete, Blinken and Polly.

You can say good-bye to them too.

Bye all three of you and good-bye to your friends. Thanks for sharing.

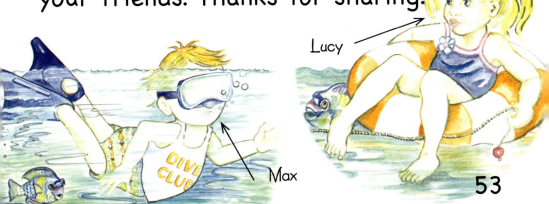

About the Author

Author and illustrator, Bonnie Staryk, lives in Marathon, a palm tree and sun-filled island in the Florida Keys. Here, she has owned and operated retail stores for fashion and home decor for over 30 years. Her previous career was in education, heading an English and Art Department at a Vermont high school and working as a pre-school Head Start Teacher in the summers. All the while she continued to cultivate her artistic endeavors.

Now retired, Bonnie, as a grandmother, has returned full-time to her love of writing and illustrating with the first in a series of children's books featuring "her" island critters. Themes of being proud of who you are and what you can do are reinforced in the humorous tales and pictures of Blinken, Pete and Polly for ages 2-6. Enjoy.